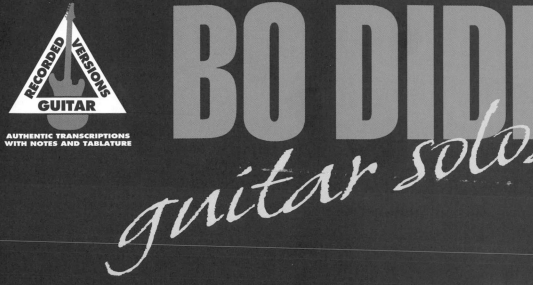

BO DIDDLEY
guitar solos

RECORDED VERSIONS
GUITAR

AUTHENTIC TRANSCRIPTIONS
WITH NOTES AND TABLATURE

Transcribed and annotated by Fred Sokolow

ISBN 978-1-4234-6413-6

ARC
MUSIC
GROUP

EXCLUSIVELY DISTRIBUTED BY

HAL•LEONARD®
CORPORATION

7777 W. BLUEMOUND RD. P.O. BOX 13819 MILWAUKEE, WI 53213

Visit Hal Leonard Online at
www.halleonard.com

ALPHABETICAL INDEX

CHRONOLOGICAL INDEX

INTRODUCTION

Bo Diddley, a.k.a. Ellas McDaniel, was born in December of 1928 on a small sharecropper's farm south of McComb, Mississippi, to a woman named Ethel Wilson. He was given the name Otha Ellas Bates (his father, whom he never knew, was named Bates) but was raised by his mother's cousin Gussie McDaniel, and he became Ellas Bates McDaniel.

Photo: University of Mississippi Blues Archive

Gussie moved Bo and her three other children to Chicago when Bo was about seven. The Baptist church Gussie took him to every Sunday provided Bo's first musical experience: the church music director taught him violin and trombone. (Bo continued to study violin for twelve years, but eventually stopped because he saw no future for a black violinist.) But when the young Bo peeked through storefront windows at Pentecostal services, he saw a different kind of music – one that made folks jump around and shout. It opened his eyes to the raw power music could have over people.

The teenage Ellas McDaniel, nicknamed "Bo Diddley" by his school friends, heard John Lee Hooker on the radio doing "Boogie Chillen," and he decided to learn to play guitar. His sister bought him a guitar and he "invented" an easy open tuning – the D or E tuning used by so many Mississippi Delta blues guitarists.

By the early 1940s, the young teen Bo was leading his own musical street corner groups (and doing some occasional amateur boxing.) Bo quit school at the age of sixteen and held several jobs, but he continued to play on the streets. To get playing pointers he would hide behind the cigarette machine at the bar where Muddy Waters played and study the reigning king of the Chicago blues scene.

By the end of the 1940s, Chicago was the blues capital of the world, with Muddy Waters, Howlin' Wolf, Little Walter, and other now-legendary blues performers playing in the local clubs. Bo was married and working at a construction job, but his street group started getting occasional gigs in clubs. He was now working with musicians who would make the classic Bo Diddley records: guitarist Jody Williams, drummer Frank Kirkland, harp player Billy Boy Arnold, and Jerome Green on maracas.

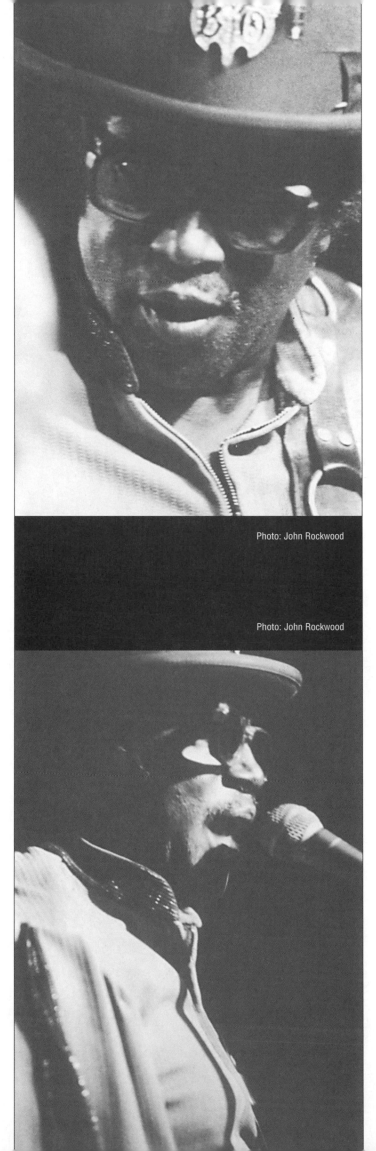

Photo: John Rockwood

Photo: John Rockwood

In 1954, Bo bought an electric guitar and he and his group started working regularly in clubs. Arnold, the harmonica player, convinced Bo to cut a demo and look for a record deal. They cut the blues tune "I'm a Man," an original of Bo's that was similar in style to Muddy Waters, and an off-color tune with an odd junglebeat that was to become "Bo Diddley," the first hit to feature Bo's signature "shave-and-a-haircut-two-bits" (♩♫♩♩|♩♩♪|).

Photo: University of Mississippi Blues Archive

The famous "Bo Diddley Beat" has been described as Latin, Caribbean, and African. In Louisiana (very near McComb, where Bo was born), a similar feel is called the "second line" rhythm. The classic rural blues tune "Hambone," along with a whole body of similar tunes often sung with only a hand-slapping-thigh accompaniment, has the same beat as, and a lyric reminiscent of, "Bo Diddley" ("Hambone, Hambone, have you heard/Papa gonna buy me a mocking bird").

Whatever its origin, Bo Diddley's beat was a novelty in the Chicago blues scene in the early 1950s (when Bo "invented" it) and was a new sound to the R&B world when "Bo Diddley" hit the charts. However, it was also unlike anything Ewart Abner of Vee Jay Records had heard when Bo brought it to him, and he rejected it, calling it "jungle music." Phil and Leonard Chess, whose Chess label was recording all the blues giants, decided to give it a try on their subsidiary Checker label (after convincing Bo to rewrite the lyric which, according to Arnold, would still be unplayable on the radio today.)

On these and subsequent sides, Diddley's band was augmented by some of the Chess "regulars," most of whom are now blues legends, like pianist Otis Spann and bassist/songwriter Willie Dixon. The sound was pure Bo Diddley. By 1955, when "I'm a Man" and "Bo Diddley" hit #2 on the R&B charts, Bo was already playing loud through two Fender Bassman amps with extra speakers added. He used lots of echo and invented a tremolo unit out of clock parts that he used on nearly all his hits. (Later in the 1950s and 1960s, many amps with names like Tremolux and Vibrolux included a built-in tremolo unit. The tremolo effect is a rapid loud/soft oscillation of variable speed and intensity.)

Photo: John Rockwood

Photo: John Rockwood

Diddley had a series of R&B smash hits with Checker. Though only a few tunes ("Crackin' Up" and "Say Man") dented the pop charts, Diddley had an immediate impact on white audiences and performers. Early in his career, Elvis caught Bo's act at the Apollo Theater; he had to have been impressed by Diddley's flamboyant stage act (the square guitar, loud clothes, phallic guitar maneuvers, etc.). Buddy Holly copied the Bo Diddley beat in his song "Not Fade Away," and so did Duane Eddy ("Cannonball"), Johnny Otis ("Willie and the Hand Jive") and Dee Clark ("Hey Little Girl"). On the R&B front, "I'm a Man" inspired Muddy Waters' "Mannish Boy," and Little Walter imitated Bo's sound with the tunes "Roller Coaster" and "Hate to See You Go" – he even included a tremolo guitar sound.

The hits continued into the early 1960s, along with TV appearances and tours throughout the U.S. and Europe. Bo's albums covered every American fad: *Surfin' with Bo Diddley, Bo Diddley's Hootenanny, Bo Diddley's a Twister, Bo Diddley Is a Gunslinger.* He also recorded an LP with Chuck Berry and two LPs with Muddy Waters (*Super Blues*, which also included Little Walter, and *Super Super Blues*, with Howlin' Wolf).

By the mid-1960s, Bo's career slowed down. Musical trends were changing and Bo Diddley could not get a hit record. His influences were stronger than ever on the rock scene. In Europe, his tunes were recorded by the Rolling Stones and the Yardbirds; Eric Burdon and the Animals recorded a song called "The Story of Bo Diddley." In the U.S. the psychedelic rock scene was going strong. San Francisco-based bands like Quicksilver Messenger Service and the Grateful Dead made Bo Diddley tunes a regular part of their repertoire (Quicksilver played "Mona" and the Dead made the Diddley beat an integral part of their sound).

In 1972 and 1973, Bo Diddley appeared in two movies: *Let the Good Times Roll* and *Keep on Rockin'*. But the 1970s brought no big upswing to Diddley's career. The Chess company was sold and Diddley began making his own records. He opened for the Clash on their 1979 English tour.

Bo continued to play clubs and concerts with the old Bo Diddley spirit until he fell ill in 2007. He was often joined onstage by his daughter, Tammi. He appeared in the 1987 movie about Chuck Berry (his friend and Chess Records companion) *Hail! Hail! Rock 'n' Roll*. Five decades after his first hit tunes were released, his legend continues:

■ He was one of rock's first innovators. His sound and style influenced other early giants like Elvis and Buddy Holly. His flamboyant appearance and exaggerated stage movements are a standard part of rock today.

■ He was the first guitar hero of rock. Odd-shaped guitars and dramatic guitar gesturing are typical today; Bo was the pioneer. More importantly, he was the first to base his personal guitar sound on loud amplification and electronic effects – pointing the way for Jimi Hendrix and later generations of heavy metal guitarists.

■ The "Bo Diddley beat" is still alive and well in pop music.

Here is close look at Bo Diddley's guitar style, beginning with an introductory overview and followed by note-for-note transcriptions of his biggest hits.

Photo: John Rockwood

Bo Diddley's Guitar Style

OPEN TUNING

When you re-tune the guitar to an "open tuning" you can play a tonic chord by strumming the "open" (unfretted) strings. Bo Diddley almost always re-tunes to an open E chord; occasionally he uses the open D tuning which is identical to open E but two frets (a whole step) lower. He plays the same chord fingerings and scale patterns in both tunings (the letter/names of the notes and chords in D tuning are a whole step below those in E tuning).

Many early blues guitarists used the open D and E tunings, especially players from the Mississippi Delta, where Bo spent the first seven years of his life: Skip James, Robert Johnson, Mississippi Fred McDowell and Muddy Waters are a few prominent examples. And, as mentioned earlier, Bo in his teen years (when he was getting his own street music bands together) watched Waters closely. Still, Bo Diddley's guitar style is truly unique and distinctive. It's only redolent of Muddy Waters on blues numbers like *I'm A Man* and *Oh Yea.*

Here's the open E tuning and the open D tuning (sometimes called the "Sebastopol" tuning).

	OPEN D TUNING	**OPEN E TUNING**
1st string:	D	E
2nd string:	A	B
3rd string:	F#	G#
4th string:	D	E
5th string:	A	B
6th string:	D	E

To get to OPEN E tuning from standard tuning:

— Tune the 4th string up to E; match it with the open 6th and 1st strings or with the 5th string/7th fret.

— Tune the 5th string up to B; match it with the open 2nd string or with the 6th string/7th fret.

— Tune the 3rd string up to G#; match it with the retuned 4th string/4th fret.

Now, you have duplicated the standard tuning/1st position E chord, tuning the 3rd, 4th and 5th strings up to the notes you normally get by fretting them:

E

To get to OPEN D tuning from standard tuning:

— Tune the 6th string down to D; match it with the 4th string. When tuned correctly, the 6th string/7th fret matches the open 5th string.

— Tune the 3rd string down to F#; match it with the 4th string/4th fret.

— Tune the 2nd string down to A; match it with the open 5th string or with the re-tuned 3rd string/3rd fret.

— Tune the 1st string down to D; match it with the open 6th and 4th strings or with the re-tuned 2nd string/5th fret.

CHORDS

Here are the first position and barred chords Diddley plays. The chord names below are for E tuning; transpose down a whole step for D tuning (e.g. in D tuning the first position A chord is a G chord).

CHORD VAMPS AND RHYTHM PATTERNS

With the exception of a few twelve-bar blues tunes *(Road Runner, She's Fine, She's Mine)*, most of Diddley's songs are one-chord *vamps* (repeated rhythmic figures) with an occasional IV, V or ♭VII chord added to the two- or four-bar pattern. For example:

The *Bo Diddley Beat* is not one distinct guitar rhythm pattern; Bo played it many different ways in tunes like *Bo Diddley, Mona, Bo's Guitar* and *Gunslinger*. The groove is immediately indentifiable, but the guitar chops vary:

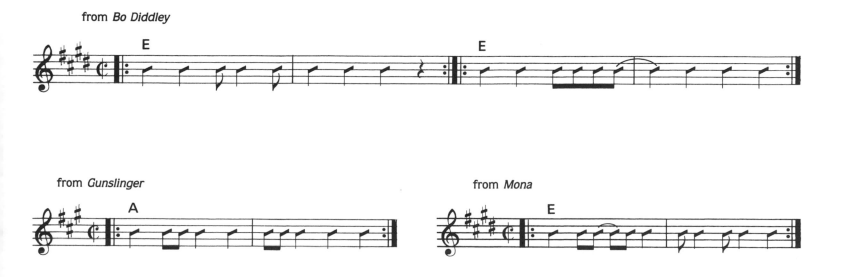

BLUES BACKUP RIFFS

In *You Don't Love Me (You Don't Care)*, *I'm A Man*, *Bring It To Jerome*, *Oh Yea* and *Diddy Wah Diddy*, Diddley plays variations of a standard blues backup riff derived from the playing of Muddy Waters and John Lee Hooker. Hooker would play it like this (in standard tuning):

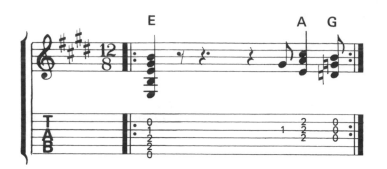

Here's the same lick the way Bo Diddley plays it in *I'm A Man* (in open E tuning):

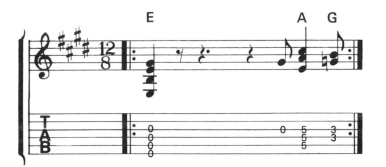

Here are some of Diddley's variations of the same lick. Each one is a rhythm part for all or most of a tune:

from *You Don't Love Me (You Don't Care)*   from *Diddy Wah Diddy*

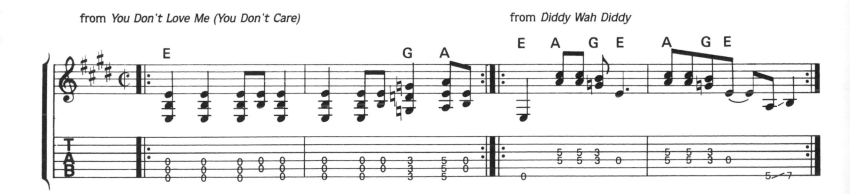

from *Bring It To Jerome*

BASS BACKUP RIFFS

Diddley often plays a repetitious bass riff throughout a tune to accompany his singing or to back up a harmonica solo. Here are some examples:

from *You Don't Love Me (You Don't Care)*   from *She's Fine, She's Mine*

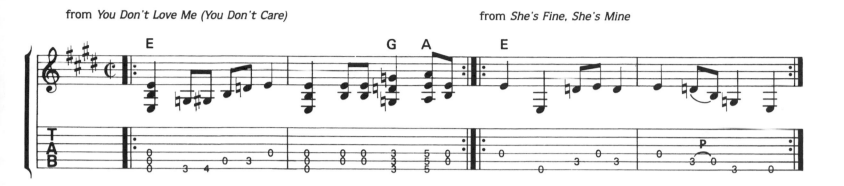

from *Oh Yea*   from *Diddley Daddy*

from *Road Runner*

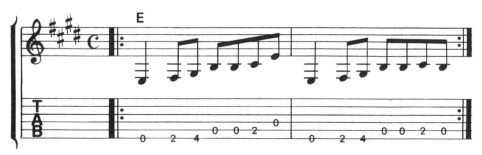

CHORD SOLOS

Some Bo Diddley solos consist of heavy first-position chord bashing (Pete Townshend of The Who, and other power-trio guitarists of the '60s obviously took notice). *Hey! Bo Diddley*, *Bo's Guitar* and *Mumblin' Guitar* provide many examples, like those below:

from *Bo's Guitar*

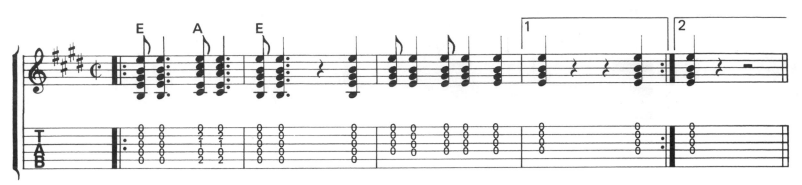

from *Hey! Bo Diddley*

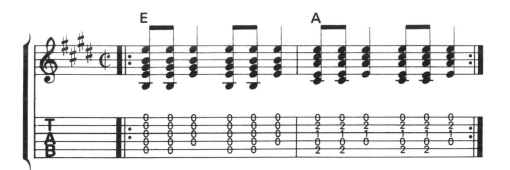

During the first-position chord solos in *Bo's Guitar* and *Bo Diddley*, Diddley plays a IV-to-V-chord sliding lick:

from *Bo Diddley*   from *Bo's Guitar*

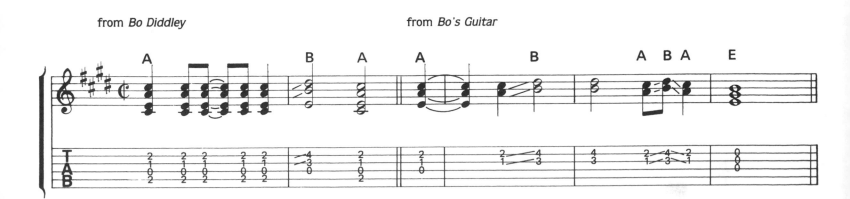

Diddley also plays power-chord solos on barred chords, often bouncing back and forth between the I and ♭VII or I and IV chords. Look at solos in *Mona, Mumblin' Guitar, Bo Diddley* and *Hey! Bo Diddley* for examples. Here are a few:

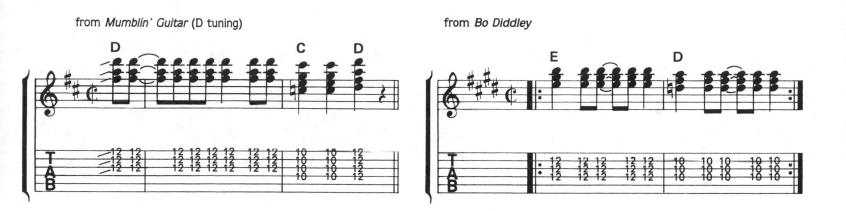

from *Mumblin' Guitar* (D tuning)

from *Bo Diddley*

from *Hey! Bo Diddley*

SINGLE NOTE SOLOING

Most of Bo Diddley's single-note soloing is based on this first-position blues scale:

Look for single-note licks and extended solos in *Who Do You Love, You Don't Love Me (You Don't Care), Diddy Wah Diddy* and *Bo's Guitar*. Here are some sample licks that illustrate Diddley's use of the blues scale:

from *Who Do You Love*

SPECIAL TECHNIQUES

Diddley's solos are often punctuated by bizarre electronic sounds or unusual guitar effects:

— On *Road Runner, Sad Sack* and *Mumblin' Guitar* he creates a screeching metal sound by sliding the side of his flatpick up or down the length of a wound string (4th, 5th or 6th string). This even makes a scraping noise on an unamplified guitar; the effect is exaggerated with high amplification and reverb. It's a standard technique among heavy metal guitarists of the '80s.

— On *Sad Sack* he beats out a conga-drum rhythm on his guitar pickup, striking it percussively with his flatpick point. This makes a metallic, popping noise.

— Also on *Sad Sack*, Diddley picks the strings *behind the capo*; the notes are random in pitch and have an odd, harmonic pinging sound.

— On *Bo's Guitar*, he picks Afro/Cuban rhythms on a single string/harmonic.

— On *Mumblin' Guitar* and *Road Runner* he executes swift, careless, swooping slides on the 6th string, well above the 12th fret, often fretting the string "overhand" like a steel guitar or Dobro player.

— Diddley's electronic effects have already been mentioned: His loud volume, heavy reverb and tremolo are an important part of his trademark sound. He now has an envelope filter (with a "wah-wah" sound) and other effects developed in the '60s and '70s built into his guitar.

— Diddley still plays a rectangular guitar; it's a replica of the Gretsch he made famous, made by Nashville luthier Tom Holmes.

The transcriptions that follow give you an in-depth look at what Bo Diddley played on eighteen of his biggest recorded hits. His impact on the rock music scene has been widely noted; this is the first detailed survey of his guitar style. It's an amazing melding of rural Mississippi Delta blues, urban Chicago blues, '50's R&B, space-age electronics and, above all, the unique personality of Bo Diddley—one of the main inventors of Rock and Roll.

Playing Guide

The songs in this collection include the vocal line, lyric, chords, rhythm guitar part, and transcribed guitar solo. In addition, a line of tablature is given directly below the notated guitar part to indicate where the notes are to be played. In the tablature example below, each line represents a single string beginning with the top line 1st string down to the bottom 6th string. Numbers placed on the lines give the fret number.

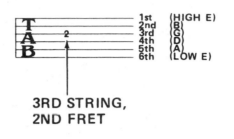

3RD STRING,
2ND FRET

Notation

There are several types of symbols found in the solos and rhythm guitar parts which represent various playing techniques. The following is an explanation of their meaning.

Choke—A slur mark below a number means that a lower note is fretted and choked or stretched up to the notated pitch. Place your finger on the fret indicated by the first number in the TAB line. Bend up to the pitch of the connected number to the right.

Example: play 7th fret/3rd string D, bend up to E

Hammer-on and pull-off—The slur mark is used to indicate a hammer-on or pull-off.

Example: play 8th fret/2nd string G, hammer-on to 10th fret 2nd string A

Example: play 8th fret/3rd string Eb, pull off to 7th fret D, then to 5th fret C

Slide—There are four possible slides. The type of slide depends on the location and direction of the line to the notehead. Slide up to the note or down to the note by one fret when the line precedes the note. A line following the note indicates a slide up or down after the note has been played.

Example: play 11th fret/2nd string
        A♯ and slide down to
        10th fret A

Example: play 9th fret/2nd string
        A♭ and slide up to 10th
        fret A

The slide after a note has been played does not end on a specific pitch. Begin lifting your finger after sliding two frets so that the string is eventually muted.

Example: play 12th fret/3rd string
        G and slide up

Example: play 12th fret/3rd string
        G and slide down

Slide to a specific note—A line connecting two notes indicates a slide from the first to the second note.

Example: play 8th fret/2nd string
        G and slide up to 10th
        fret A

Example: play 10th fret/1st string
        D and slide down to 8th
        fret C

Tremolo—This notation indicates very rapid up-and-down-strokes with the flatpick, mandolin style (not the electronic effect):

Harmonics—Pick a string while touching it lightly (not fretting it) at a designated fret, just over the fretwire. This produces a bell-like tone.

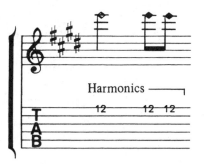

Shake—Make a sustaining tremolo effect by shaking the hand, from the wrist, while fretting a note.

Arpeggio—Pick up or down slowly on the chord, one note (string) at a time, creating a harp-like arpeggio.

String-Scratching—Slide the side of a flatpick up or down the length of a wound string (4th, 5th or 6th string), to create a scraping, scratching noise. The notation with numbers indicates approximately where the pick slides.

Muted Strings or Chords—Pick a string or chord that is to be muted or damped; mute it by touching the string (or strings) with the left hand, but not fretting it, to deaden the sound. The pitch of the half-muted string is slightly audible, so a specific fret position is indicated.

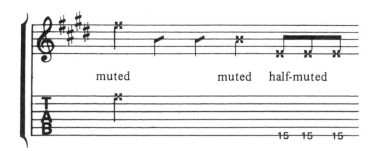

BO DIDDLEY

Since he's singing and playing at the same time, Diddley's guitar pattern keeps changing in response to his vocal line. The groove is relentless, in spite of these variations.

A two-bar vocal line is "answered" by a two-bar guitar phrase. This pattern is repeated in other Bo Diddley hits (such as *Hey! Bo Diddley*).

Words and Music by
ELLAS McDANIEL

E tuning
Capo up 3 frets (Actual key: G)

Bright "Bo Diddley" beat

Bo Did - dley-'ll buy his ba-by a dia - mond ring.__

If that dia - mond ring __ don't shine, __

he gon - na take it to a pri - vate eye.__

If that pri - vate eye can't see,

he bet-ter not take the ring__ from me.

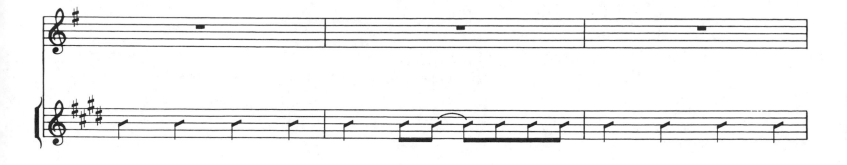

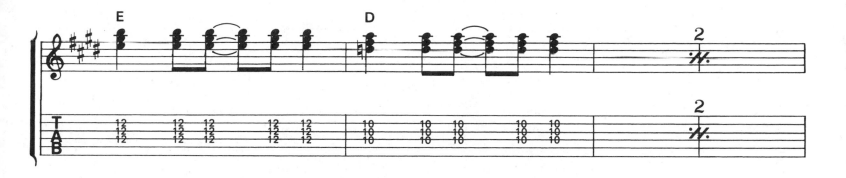

Bo Did - dley caught a nan - ny goat

to make his pret - ty ba - by a Sun - day coat.

Bo Did-dley caught a

bear - cat to

make his pret - ty ba - by a Sun - day hat.

Repeat 4 times

26

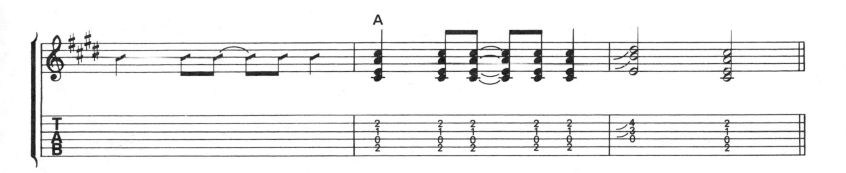

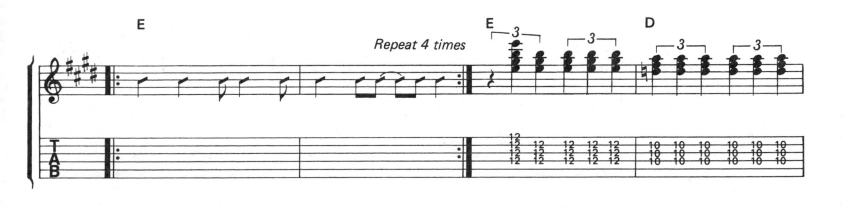

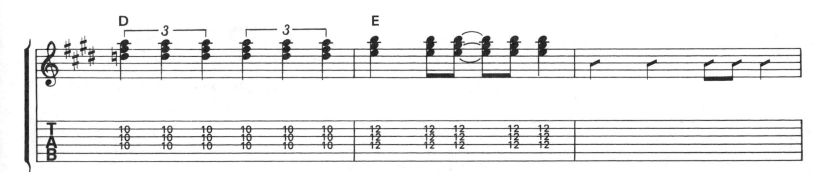

27

28

gone a-gain.

Bo Did-dley, Bo Did-dley, have you heard?

My pret-ty ba-by said she was a bird.

Repeat 4 times

E   D   E   Repeat and fade

I'M A MAN

Simple and powerful, Diddley's first release is one of his most-recorded tunes. It has been covered by blues artists Muddy Waters, Ko Ko Taylor, John Hammond and Eric Clapton as well as The Yardbirds, The Who, The Royal Guardsmen, Doug Sahm, Fabian, Cheech and Chong and others!

It took about thirty takes to get the original *I'm A Man* recorded, because the Chess brothers kept telling Diddley to spell *man*, but were unable to express *musically* what they wanted. Finally the weary and angry Diddley said it exaggeratedly slowly: "M . . . A . . . N," which is what Phil and Leonard Chess were looking for all along.

E tuning
Capo on 3rd fret (Actual key: G)

Words and Music by
ELLAS McDANIEL

Man.___ Ah,_____ ah,_____

ah,_____ ah._____ All you pret-ty wom-en

stand in line.___ I can make love to you, ba-by, in a hour's_time.

I'm a man,___ spelled M._____ A.___

N.___ Man.___ *(Harp solo)*

I'm go-in' back down ___ to Kan-sas soon, bring back the sec - ond cou-sin,

Lit-tle John the Con-quer-oo. I'm a man,___ spelled M.

A.___ N.___ Man.___

Ohh,_____ ohh._____ The line I shoot

D. S. and fade

will nev-er miss. The way I make love___ to 'em, they can't re-sist.

DIDDLEY DADDY

Vocal backup is by the Moonglows, a popular R&B vocal group of the '50s. This time they answer the two-bar vocal line, instead of Diddley's guitar answering.

Words and Music by ELLAS McDANIEL
and HARVEY FUQUA

E tuning

Moderately bright shuffle

(Continue 2-bar riff throughout song.)

Vocal chorus:

(Did - dley, Did - dley, Did - dley, Did - dley dad - dy.)

Repeat 4 times

I've got a ba - by that's oh, so pret - ty.
My ba - by start - ed to cry in vain.____

(Did - dley, Did - dley, dum, dum-

dum - di - Did - dley.) I found her right here____ in the wind - y cit - y.
Said, "Bo Did - dley, you know you're a nat - 'ral born man."____

BRING IT TO JEROME

The rhythm gets "turned around" in the second verse; the odd bar of 6/4 time straightens things out and puts the downbeat where it should be.

Jerome Green, the song's composer, was Bo's maracas player.

Words and Music by
JEROME GREEN

E tuning
Capo up **3** frets (Actual key: G)

Bright Blues shuffle

I won't do you no wrong.
say you got an-oth-er man.
Bring— it on

home,———
bring— it to Jer-

ome.
Bring— it on home,———

Second time, D. S. to 1st Rhythm Guitar pattern and fade

bring— it to Jer-ome.

1. Look-a here,
2. (Harmonica Solo)

36

HEY! BO DIDDLEY

A lot of chord soloing here, and another two-bar vocal/two-bar guitar-answer pattern.

Ronnie Hawkins and Bill Black (Elvis' original bass player) recorded covers of the tune.

Words and Music by
ELLAS McDANIEL

E tuning
Capo up 1 fret (Actual key: F)

Fast Country shuffle

Repeat 3 times

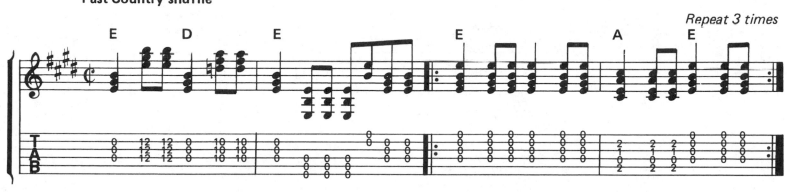

Bo Did-dle-y had a farm. (Hey! Bo Did - dley.)_

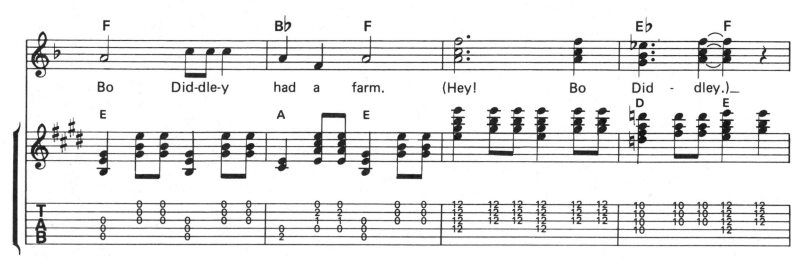

(Repeat previous 4-bar rhythm guitar throughout tune.)

On that farm there were some wom - en. (Hey! Bo

Did - dley. _) Wom - en here, wom - en there.

(Hey! Bo Did - dley. _) Wom - en, wom - en,

wom - en ev - 'ry - where, (Hey! Bo Did - dley.__) But

one lit - tle girl lived on a hill. (Hey! Bo
2. rode right up to__ my front door.
3. Saw my ba - by run a - cross the field.

Did - dley.__) She rus - tled and tus - sled like Buf - fa - lo Bill.
Knocked and knocked 'til her fists got sore.
Slip - pin' and slid - in' like an au - to - mo - bile.

(Hey! Bo Did - dley.__) One day she de - cid - ed to
When she turned and
Hol - lered at my ba - by and

go for a ride, (Hey! Bo Did - dley.__) with a
walked a - way,
told her to wait.

pis - tol and a sword by her side. (Hey! Bo
all I could hear my__ ba - by say:
Slipped off from me like a Cad - il - lac Eight.

Did - dley.__) She Hey! Bo Did - dley.__

(Hey! Bo Did - dley.__) Oh! Bo

To Coda ⊕ **D.S. al Coda**

Did - dley.__ (Oh! Bo Did - dley.__)

⊕ **CODA**

Did - dley.__) Hey! Bo Did - dley.__ (Hey! Bo Did - dley.__)

38

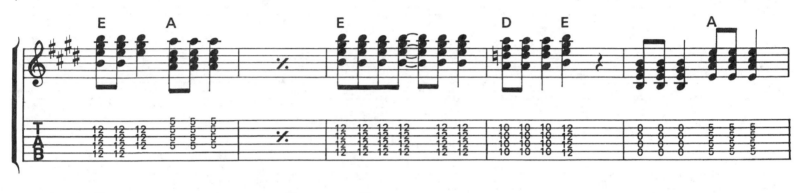

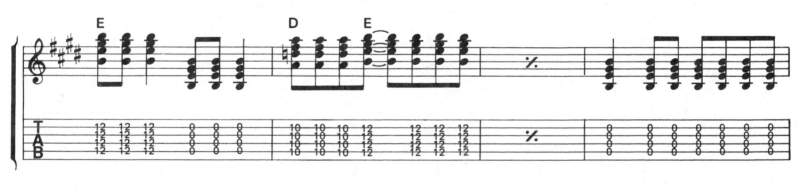

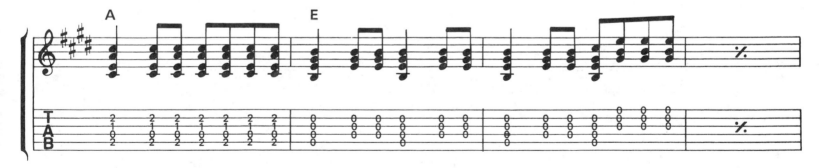

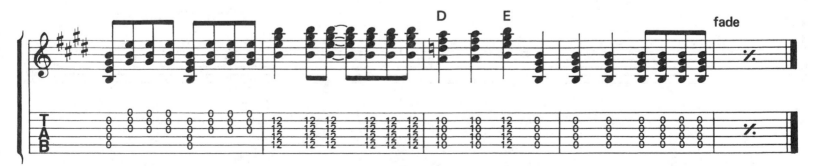

DIDDY WAH DIDDY

Notice the nice bluesy "double-bend" in the seventh and eighth bars.

Vocal backup is by the Moonglows. (The question "Just what does Diddy Wah Diddy mean?" has plagued at least two generations. The best answer, so far, came from Robert Crumb's cartoon character, Mr. Natural: "If you don't know by now, don't mess with it!").

E tuning, Tremolo
Capo up 3 frets (Actual key: G)

Words and Music by ELLAS McDANIEL
and WILLIE DIXON

wah.) This lit - tle girl, _____ she's sweet as she can be. } (Did - dy
She kiss - es me _____ all the time. _____

I got a gal down in Did - dy wah did - dy.

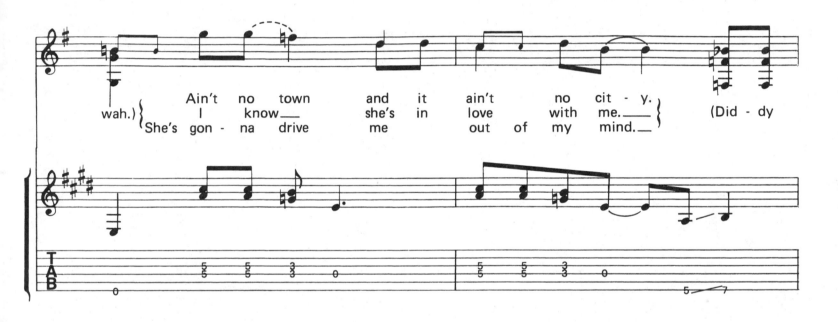

wah.) I know _____ she's in love with me. _____ (Did - dy
She's gon - na drive me out of my mind. _____

Ain't no town and it ain't no cit - y.

She'd love a man 'til it's a pit - y. Cra - zy for my gal in
wah.) The love - liest thing, she's so pret - ty, but she lives way _____ down in
An - y day, she says she's read - y to head right _____ back to
(Did - dy wah.)

G *Tacet*

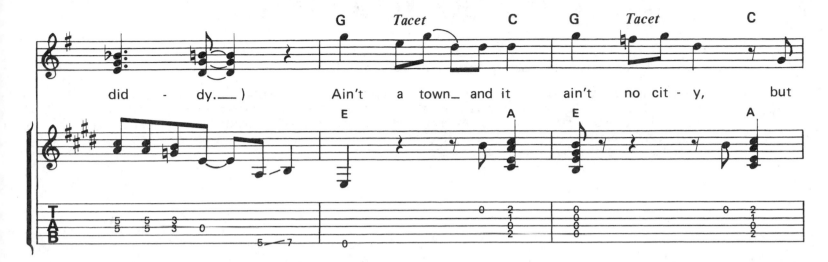

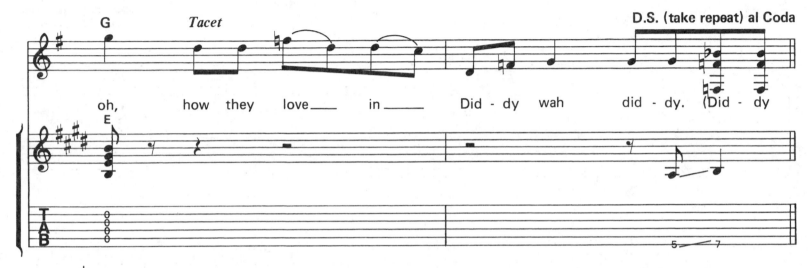

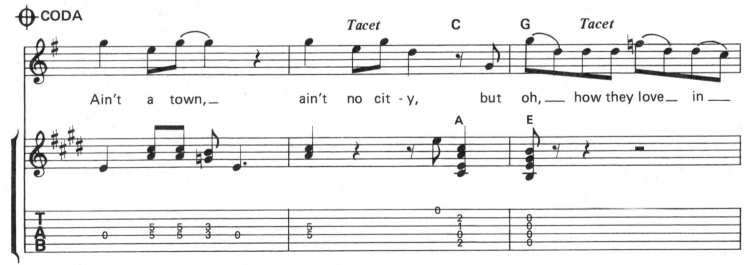

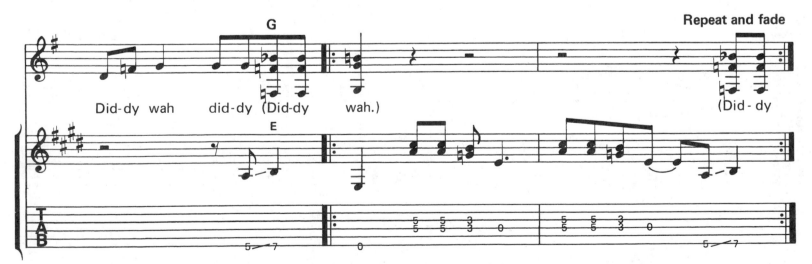

WHO DO YOU LOVE

Here are some extended single-note solos, a rarity on Diddley's vocal hits.

Who Do You Love is Diddley's "most-covered" song. Here's a partial list of the diverse legion of artists who have recorded it: George Thorogood, Townes Van Zandt, The Yardbirds, The Blues Project, Santana, John Hammond, Tom Rush, Bob Seger, Quicksilver Messenger Service, British blues/rock group Brownsville Station, The Doors, rockabilly singer Ronnie Hawkins, and The Band, who once were Hawkins' backup band. The tune is in the soundtrack of the '80s film about Richie Valens, *LA BAMBA*.

E tuning
Capo up 4 frets (Actual key: A♭)

Words and Music by
ELLAS McDANIEL

Bright Country shuffle

3.

I walk for-ty-sev-en miles of barbed wire. I use a

Ⓐ *rhythm pattern*

co - bra snake for a neck - tie. I got a

(Continue this 2-bar backup pattern throughout verse)

brand new house on the road - side made from rat - tle-snake

hide. I got a brand new chim - ney made on top,

made out of a hu - man skull. Now come on, take a lit - tle

walk with me, Ar - lene, and tell me, who do you love?

li - on to town,___ used a rat - tle - snake whip.   Take it eas - y Ar-lene, don't
𝄉 Ar - lene took me by my___ hand, she says: "Oo - ee, Bo, you know I

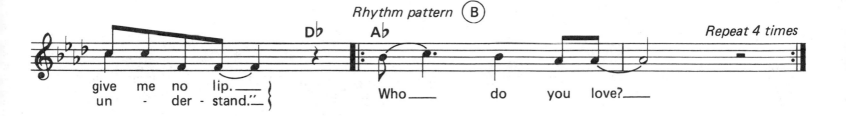

give me no lip.___   Who___ do you love?___
un - der - stand."

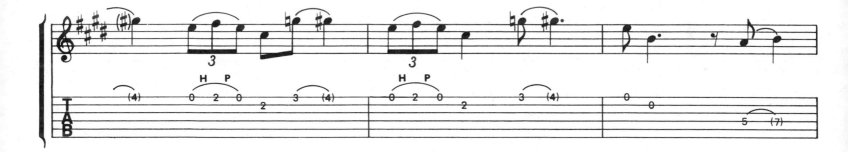

A *pattern*

Night was dark__ when the sky was blue.__ Down the al - ley a ice-

wag - on flew. Hit a bump__ and some-bod - y screamed.__

D. S. al Coda
(take repeats)

You should have heard just what I seen.__

CODA

fade

49

MONA
(I Need You Baby)

Yet another tune with a two-bar vocal followed by a two-bar answer from the guitar, *Mona* features typical Bo Diddley up-the-neck chord soloing.

E tuning. Tremolo on amp.
Capo up 3 frets (Actual key: G)

Words and Music by
ELLAS McDANIEL

Bright Bo Diddley beat

(Continue similar improvisational 2-bar rhythm pattern throughout tune.)

Hey, _____ Mo - na, _____

ooh, _____ Mo - na. _____

Yeah, yeah, _____ yeah, yeah, Mo - na. _____

Ohh, _____ Mo - na. _____

Tell you, Mo - na, what I want to do: _____

Build my house ___ next door ___ to you. _____

51

(Continue similar improvisational rhythm guitar.)

Hey,_____ hey,_____ Mo - na.__

Oh,_____ Mo - na.__

D. S. al Coda

CODA

Guitar

fade

BO'S GUITAR

With its spare melody on the treble strings, loping bass-string melody and heavy echo and tremolo, this sounds like early surf music! Note the odd, rhythmic use of a single-string harmonic.

Words and Music by ELLAS McDANIEL
and CLIFTON JAMES

E tuning

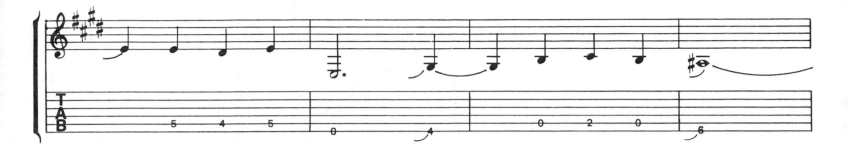

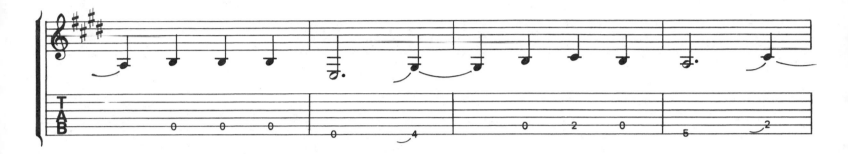

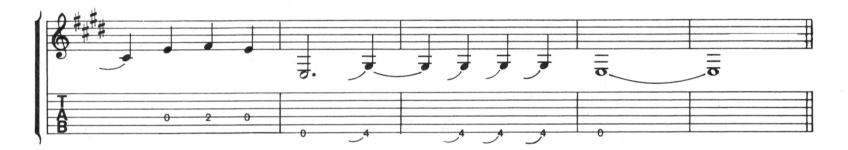

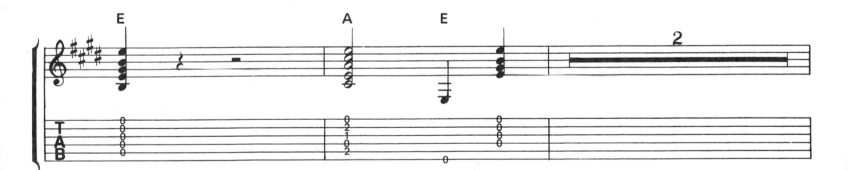

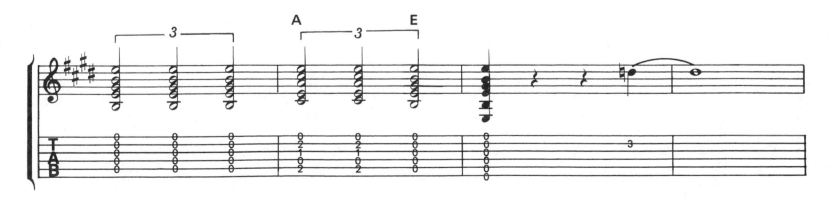

55

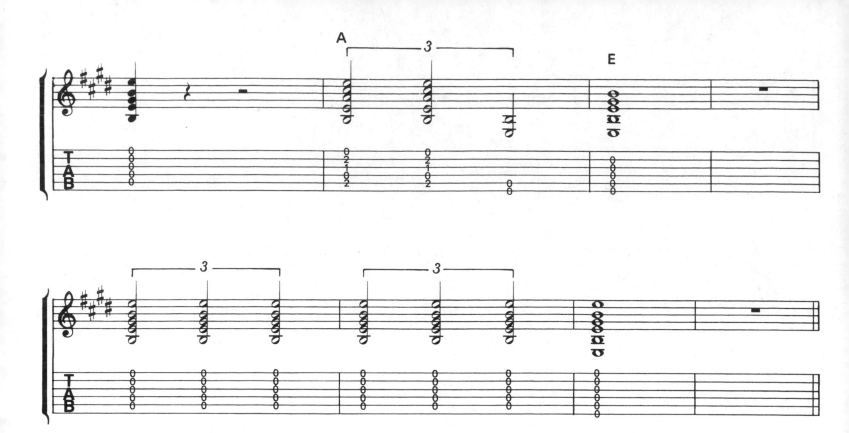

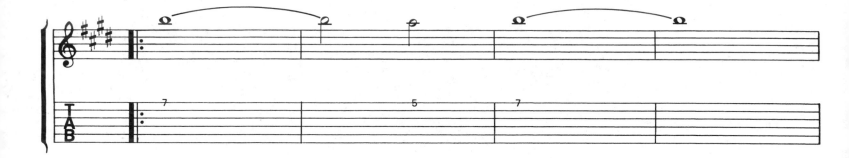

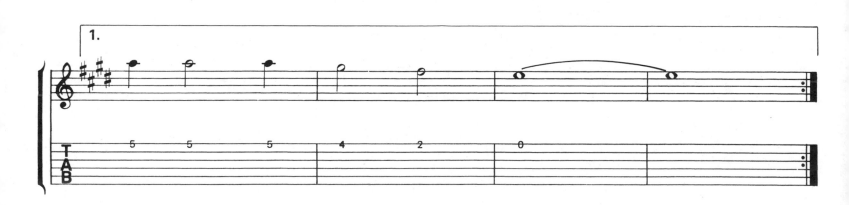

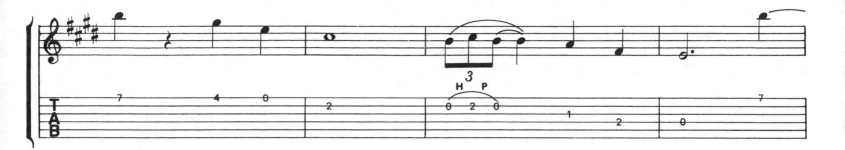

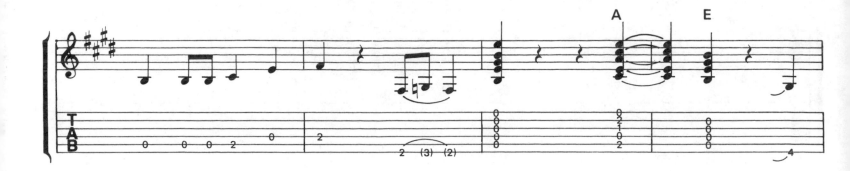

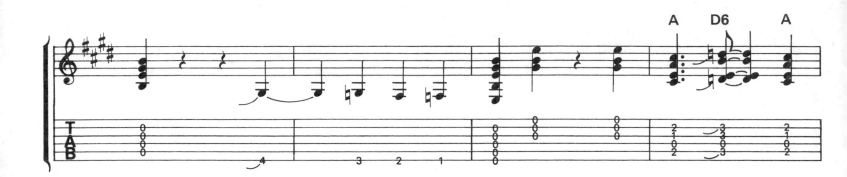

58

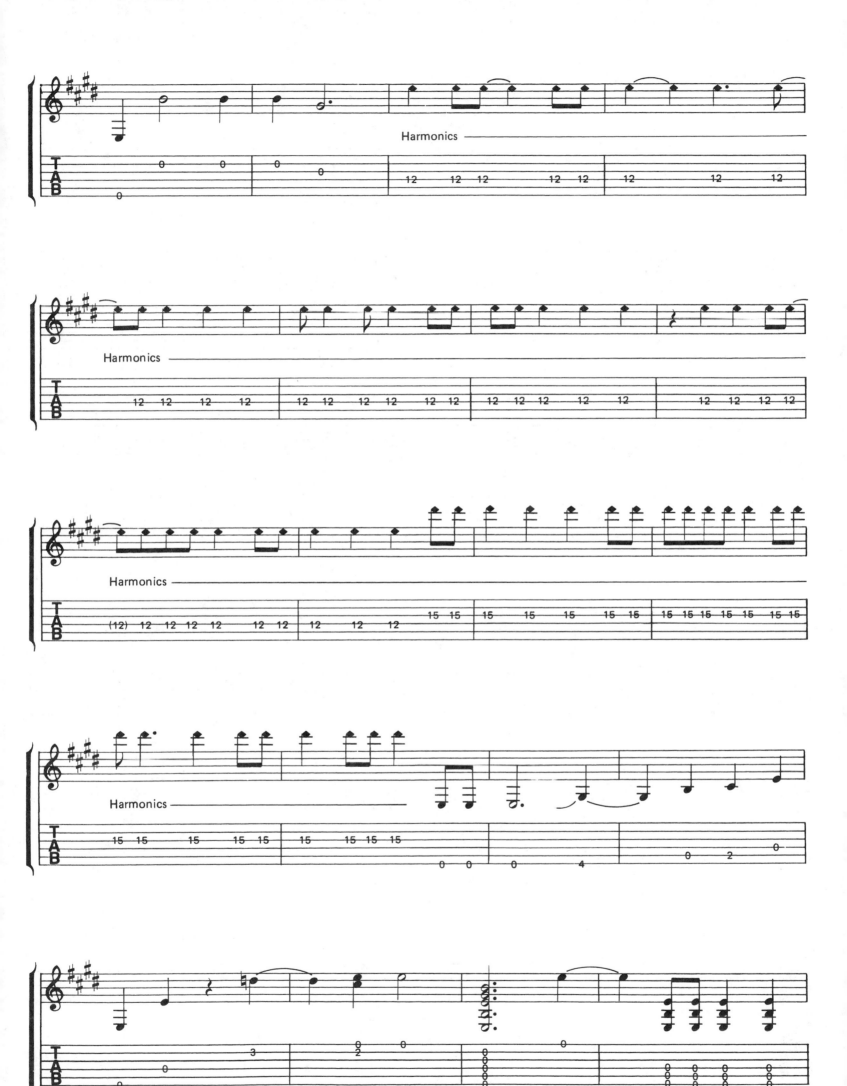

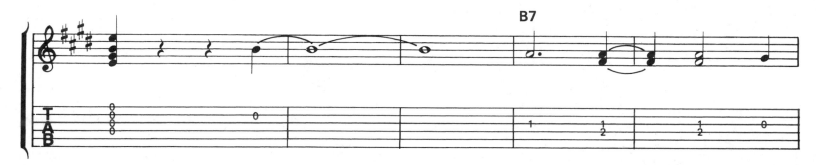

Repeat with ad lib and fade

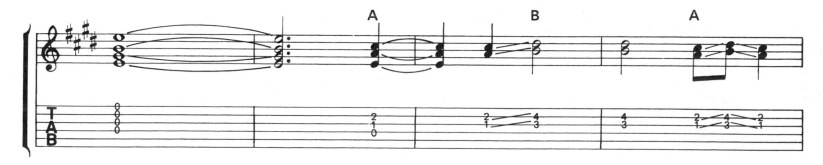

60

SAY MAN

This is not really a rap tune, because the rap doesn't rhyme or fit into the song's rhythm. Call it *proto-rap*. . .or rock 'n' roll vaudeville.

Words and Music by
ELLAS McDANIEL

D tuning

Moderate Bo Diddley beat

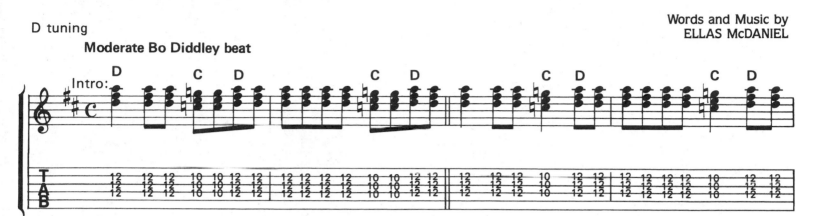

Repeat variations of the 2-bar Intro patterns above throughout spoken lyrics, then fade.

Dialogue

"Say man." "What's that, boy?" "I wanna tell you about your girlfriend."
"What about my girl." "But you don't look strong enough to take the message."
"I'm strong enough." "I might hurt your feelings." "My feelings are
already hurt by being here with you." "Well, I was walking down the
street with your girl the other day." "Uh-huh." "And the wind was blowing
real hard." "Is that right?" "And the wind blew her hair into my face."
"Uh-huh." "You know what else happened?" "What happened?" "The wind
blew her hair into her face." "Yeah." "And we went a little further. You want
to hear the rest of it?" "I'm askin' real hard." "The wind blew her hair in the street!"

"Hey, since you told me about my girl, I'm gonna tell you about yours."
"I was walkin' down the street with your girl." "Yes." "I took her home,
for a drink, you know." "Took her home?" "Yeah, just for a drink." "Oh."
"But that chick looked so ugly, she had to sneak up on the glass to get a
drink of water." "You got the nerve to call somebody ugly — why, you're so ugly
that the stork that brought you into the world ought to be arrested."
"That's alright, my mama didn't have to put a sheet over my head, so sleep
could slip up on me."

"Yeah, look-a here." "What's that?" "Where you from." "South America."
"What that?" "South America." "You don't look like no South American to
me." "I'm still from South America." "What part?" "South Texas."
"Where your Western boots at?" "I got 'em on." "Them ain't no boots
you got on, they're brogans."

"Hey, look-a here." "What's that?" "I been tryin' to figure out what you is."
"I already figured out what you is." "What's that?" "You're that thing I
throw peanuts at." "Well, look-a here." "What's that?" "You should be
ashamed of yourself." "Why?" "Calling people ugly." "I didn't call you
ugly." "What did you say?" "I said you was ruined, that's all." "You know
somethin'?" "What?" "You look like you been whupped with a ugly stick."
"Hey, I ain't got nothing to do with it, but I need a Bill of Rights."

OH YEA

Here's a variation of the *I'm A Man*-school-of-blues tunes. Vocal backup is by the Carnations.

Words and Music by
ELLAS McDANIEL

I picked up the tel-e-phone, __ and called her paw at home.

He says,"Hey, lit-tle boy, __ you bet-ter let my daugh-ter a-lone."

Rhythm Guitar lick (B)

(Continue lick (B) *)*

I says,"Oh yea?" __ He says,"Oh yea!" __ I says,"Mm - hmm?" __

He says,"You know yea." __ Her moth-er got mad and start-ed to jump and shout.

They start-ed to run down there and have the cops to car-ry me out. I says,"Oh yea?" __

She says,"Mm - hmm." __ I says,"Oh yea?" __ Her pa-pa says,"Sure 'nough." __

Repeat and fade

I said,"But I love her, I love her, __ I love her." __

CRACKIN' UP

With vocal help from the Carnations and a familiar pop "IIm-V-I" progression (very atypical of Bo Diddley), *Crackin' Up*'s smooth sound gave it entrée to the pop charts. (The bass played an F# under Bo's A chord, creating a IIm/F#m chord.) The Rolling Stones did a cover version.

The soloing consists of slight embellishments of the open E and barred E, A and B chords.

Words and Music by
ELLAS McDANIEL

E tuning

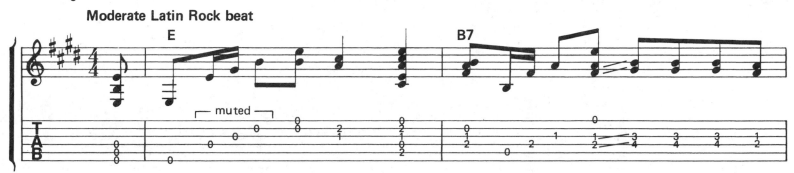

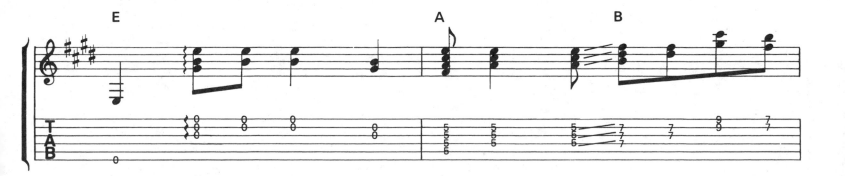

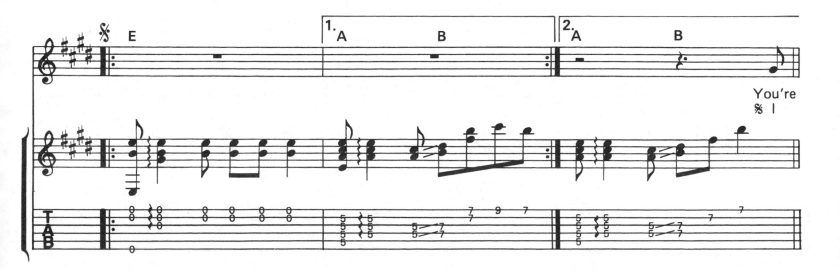

al - ways holl-'rin 'bout where I've been.__
do your laun-dry and your cook-in' too.__
spoiled you, wom-an, a long time a-go.

You're al - ways scream-in' 'bout the mon-ey I spend.__
What more, wom-an, can a man like me do?__
I used to cook your meals and bring it to your door.__

What's bug - gin' you?
You're bug - gin' me. } Yeah,
I'm all__ fed up. Yeah,

yeah, _____ you're crack-in' up.
yeah, _____ you're bug-gin' me.

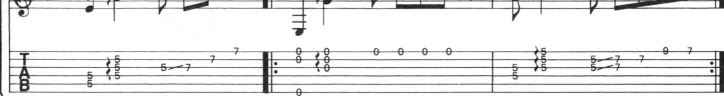

MUMBLIN' GUITAR

This instrumental consists of a two-bar "mumblin'" lick played up the neck on the 6th string (past the 12th fret) followed by an answer-back two-bar chord lick. Diddley plays two answer-back licks, one up the neck and one in first position. The 6th string licks sound like they are "mumbling" because of rapid sliding up and down the frets while Bo picks the notes; he's probably fretting the 6th string "overhand" (instead of the normal "wrist-under-the-neck" approach) which creates a sloppy, mumbling sound.

The instrumental continues on past the end of this transcription in similar manner, with occasional feedback squeaks and other odd noises in the "mumblin'" sections.

Words and Music by
ELLAS McDANIEL

D tuning

Bright Country shuffle

(Spoken:) *What you say, man? Quit mumblin', and talk out loud.*

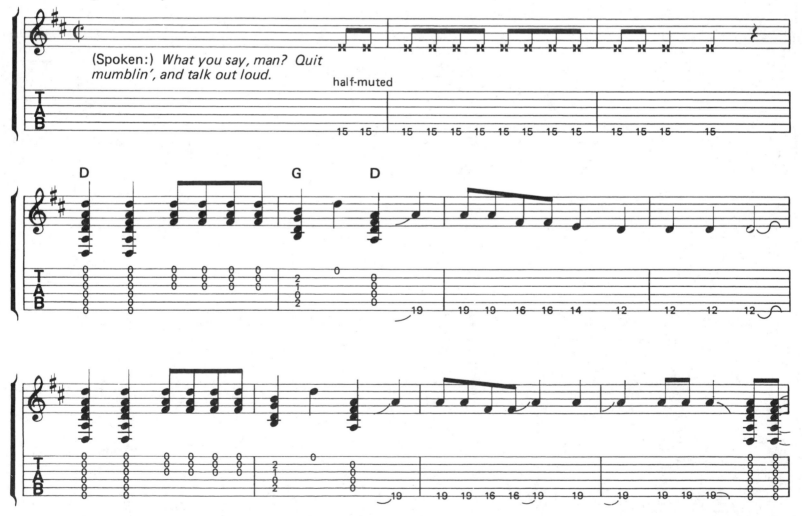

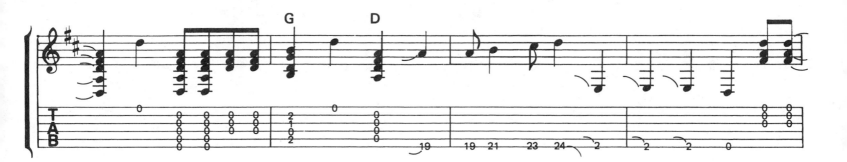

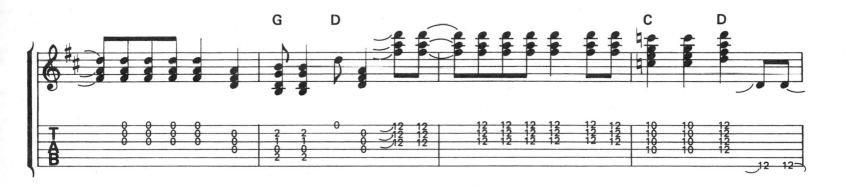

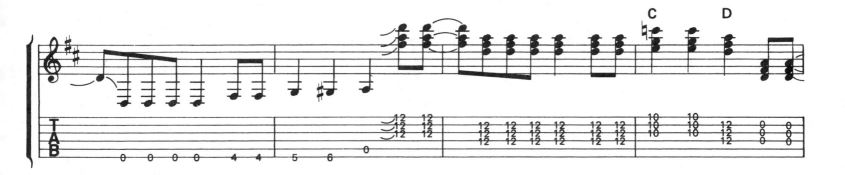

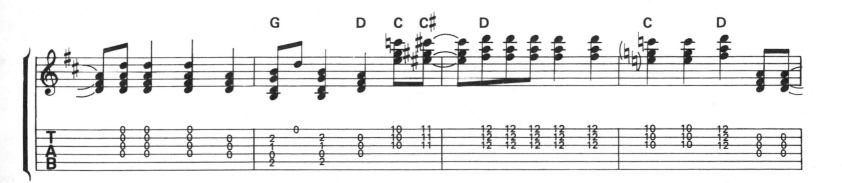

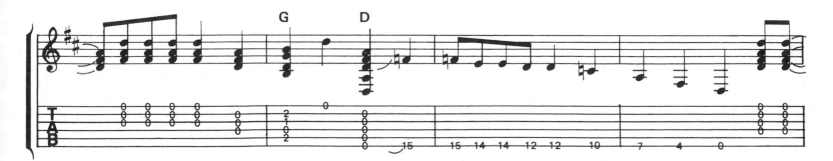

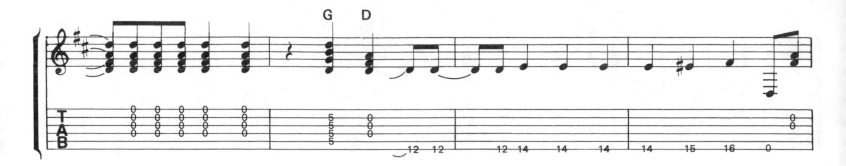

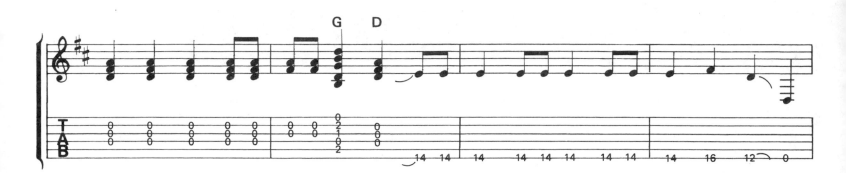

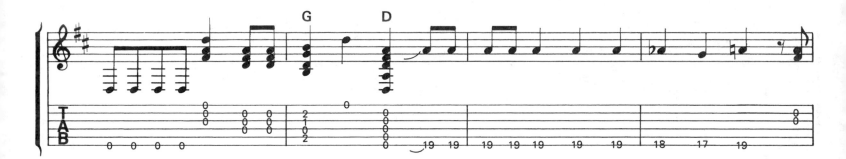

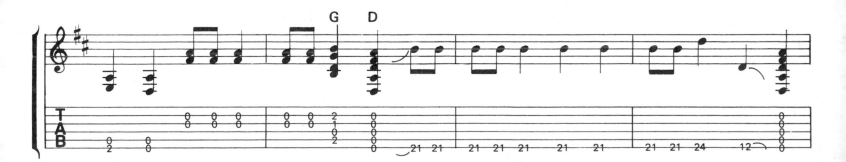

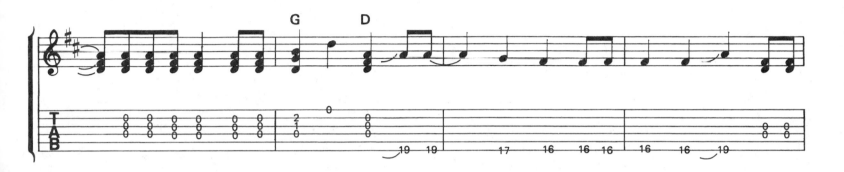

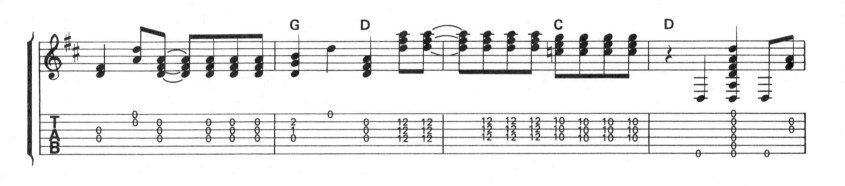

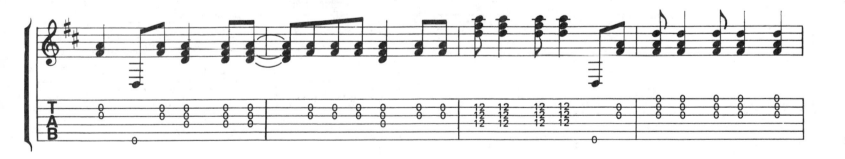

ROAD RUNNER

This is one of the few twelve-bar blues Diddley recorded. He plays a standard bass-string/boogie lick throughout, and adds a few string-scraping automotive effects. The concept of the "Roadrunner" (and the "beep beep") comes from the cartoon character of the same name.

Road Runner was recorded by surf/rock group the Ventures, and by the Royal Guardsmen, Johnny Winter, The Who, Brownsville Station and others.

Words and Music by
ELLAS McDANIEL

E tuning

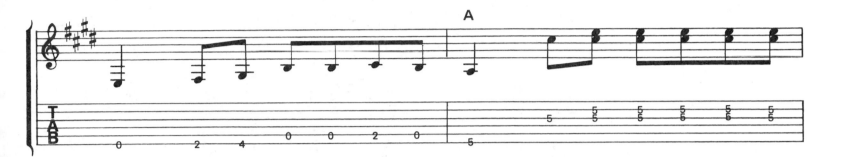

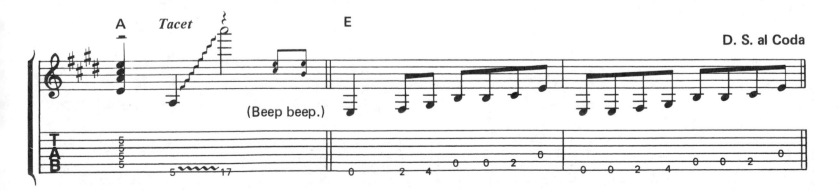

77

GUN SLINGER

In 1960, when westerns proliferated on television, Diddley penned this tune for an Lp titled BO DIDDLEY IS A GUNSLINGER. He never hesitated to take advantage of a fad; other album titles include SURFIN' WITH BO DIDDLEY and BO DIDDLEY'S BEACH PARTY. There are also fad song titles: *Limbo, Bo Diddley's Hootenanny, Bo's Twist* and even *Twisting Waves* (two fads at once)!

Warren Zevon recorded a cover version of *Gun Slinger*.

Words and Music by
ELLAS McDANIEL

E tuning
Capo up 5 frets (Actual key: A)

'bout Bo Did - dley at the O. K. Cor - ral.
streets get emp - ty and the sun goes down. (Bo Did - dley's a

gun sling - er.) Now Bo Did - dley did - n't stand no mess.
(Sher - iff ___ stand - in' in the door - way,

(Bo Did - dley's a gun sling - er.) He wore a gun on his hip ___ and a rose
you know he's so ___ scared

To Coda ⊕   **D. S. al Coda**

___ on his chest.
to say: (Bo Did - dley's a gun sling - er.)

⊕ **CODA**

gun sling - er.) Yeah, ___ uh - huh.

Oh. ___

Yeah, ___

___ yeah. Uh - huh.

Bo Did - dley's a gun sling - er. (Bo Did - dley's a

fade

gun sling - er.) Yeah, ___ uh - huh.

79

YOU DON'T LOVE ME
(You Don't Care)

Diddley repeats the same two-bar pattern (bars 7-8) throughout the tune, adding a slight variation to the pattern during the harmonica solo. The endless repetition of this bluesy lick is hypnotic.

Blues guitarist Buddy Guy and British blues/rock group Savoy Brown have recorded versions of the tune.

Words and Music by
ELLAS McDANIEL

care. You don't want me _____

Repeat 3 times

hang - in' 'round here, hang - in' 'round here.

(Continue same rhythm pattern)

Well, I love you, yes, ____ I do.
Yes, I saw you on ____ the street,
Yes, I need you, yes, ____ I do.

Ain't noth - in' in the world ____ I would - n't do for you, ____
tell - in' your man ____ you did - n't love me, ____
You know, ____ pret - ty ma - ma, what I would try for you, ____

SAD SACK

Diddley tuned to open E and capoed up 5 frets, but instead of playing in the key of A, as he normally would, he played this instrumental in D. The tonic chord is the first-position IV chord (or the barred chord five frets above the capo).

This tune starts with a straight-four rock feel, but becomes more Latin and cut-time as it progresses. Like *Bo's Guitar*, there are hints of surf-music-to-come.

His unusual guitar techniques include striking the pickup with the flatpick point for rhythmic effect; strumming and picking strings *behind the capo*; and scratching a wound string with the side of the flatpick.

Guitarist Elvin Bishop quoted a large portion of this tune during an instrumental jam on Paul Butterfield's EAST/WEST Lp.

E tuning
Capo up 5 frets (Actual key: D)

Words and Music by
ELLAS McDANIEL

Moderate Rock

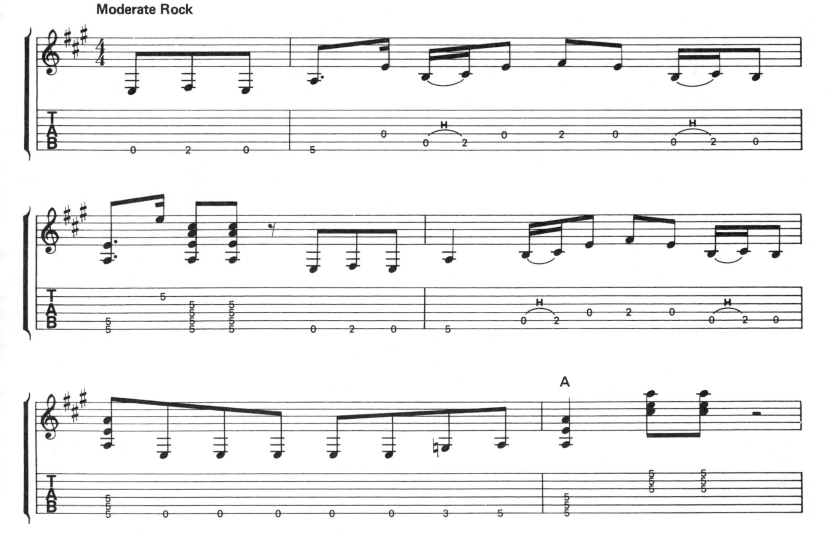

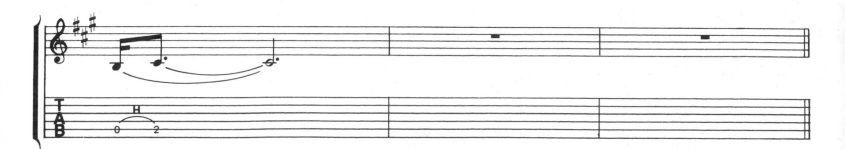

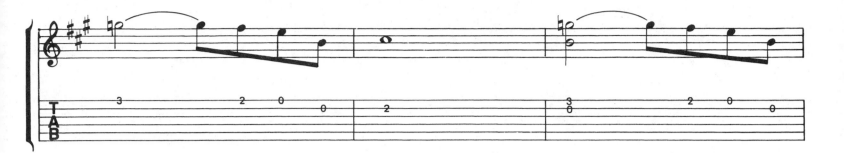

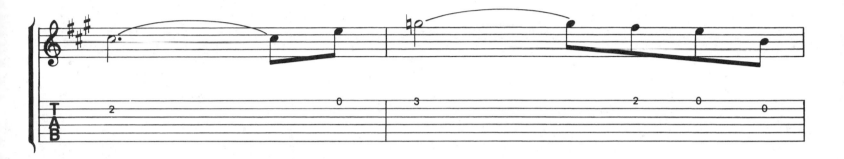

Pick behind capo

85

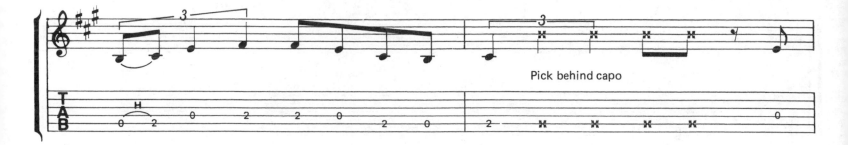

Pick behind capo

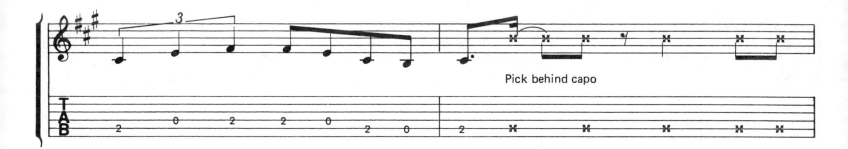

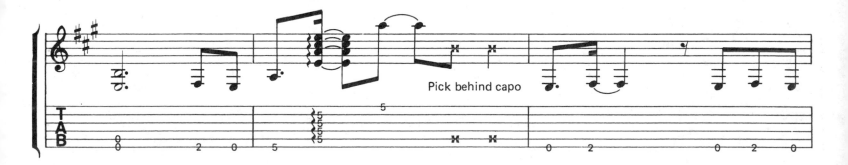

Pick behind capo

Pick behind capo

Hit pick-up with pick

Hit pick-up with pick

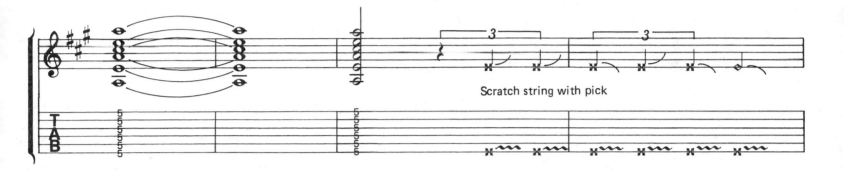

Scratch string with pick

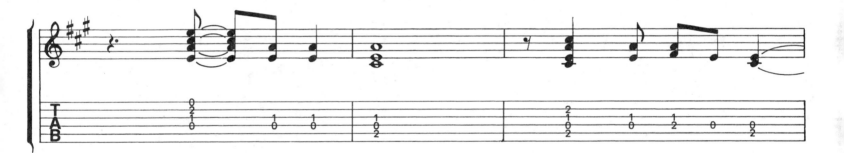

Pick behind capo

Pick behind capo

Pick behind capo

Pick behind capo

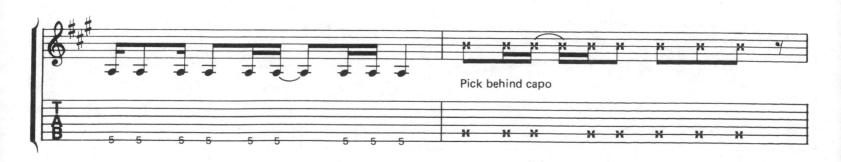

Pick behind capo

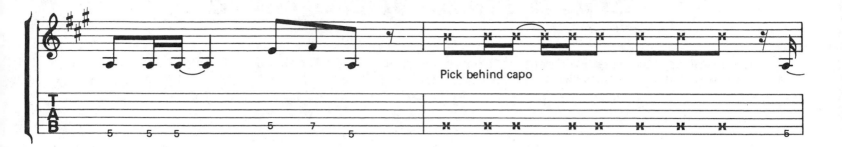

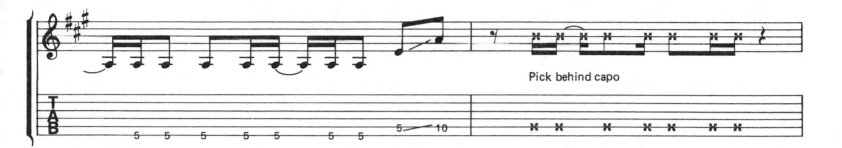

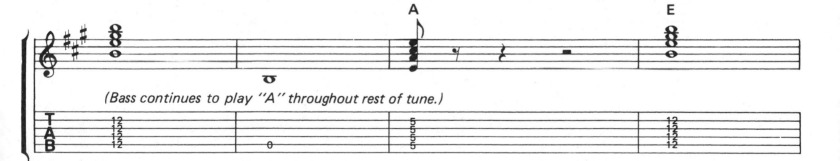

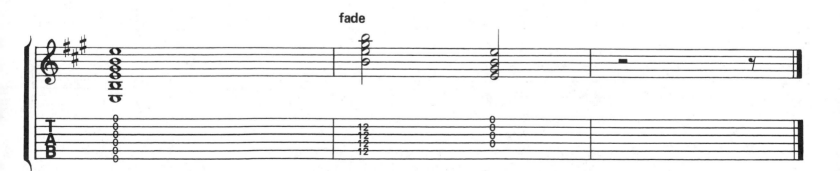

SHE'S FINE, SHE'S MINE

This twelve-bar blues creates a repetitious, bluesy hypnotic effect not unlike that of *You Don't Love (You Don't Care)*. Notice the unusual A9 chord.

E tuning
Capo up 5 frets (Actual key: A)

Moderate shuffle

Words and Music by
ELLAS McDANIEL

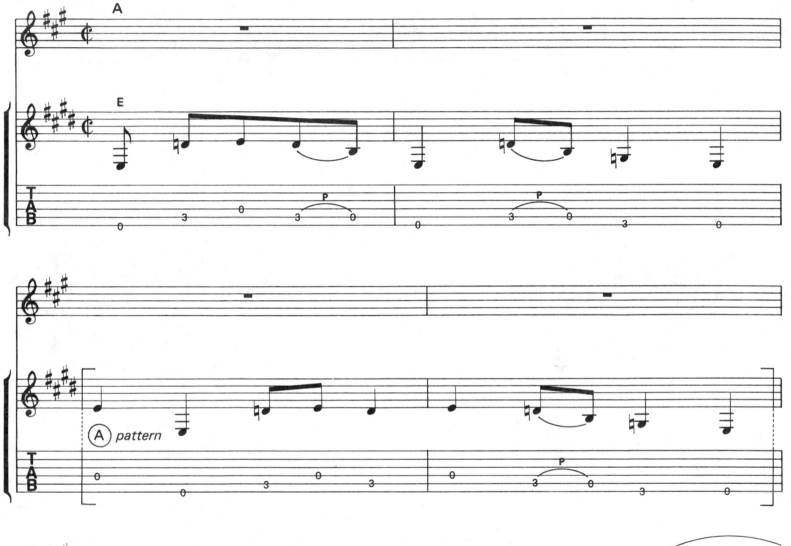

Ah,

ah.

Ah,

mm _____ ah _____ ah.

Well,— you don't love me,

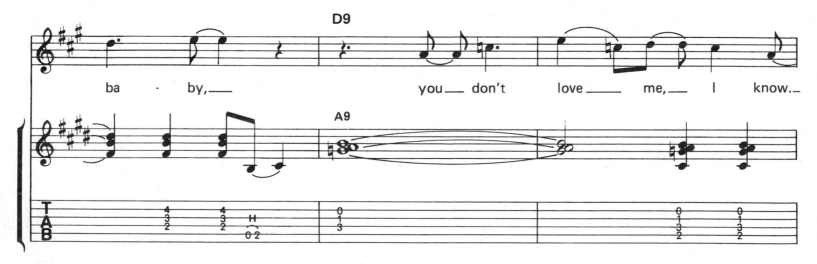

ba - by,— you— don't love— me,— I know.—

You've_ been tak - in'___
leave me;___

tak - in' all my mon - ey and my clothes._
please_ don't nev - er nev - er go. ___

You've_ been tak - in'___
Please_ don't leave me,___

DISCOGRAPHY

The 18 songs in this collection were originally released on Checker LPs, except for "Mona" and "She's Fine, She's Mine," which originally were released as singles and were not included on any albums. These tunes are now available on the compilation *The Story of Bo Diddley.* "

Bo Diddley includes the tunes "Bo Diddley," "I'm a Man," "Bring It to Jerome," "Hey! Bo Diddley," "Diddley Daddy," "Diddy Wah Diddy" and "Who Do You Love."

Go Bo Diddley includes "Crackin' Up," "Bo's Guitar," "You Don't Love Me (You Don't Care)," "Say Man" and "Oh Yea."

"Mumblin' Guitar" originally appeared on the LP *Have Guitar Will Travel.*

"Road Runner" appeared on three LPs: *Road Runner, In the Spotlight* and *Bo Diddley's Beach Party.*

"Gun Slinger" appeared on *Bo Diddley Is a Gunslinger* and *Bo Diddley's Beach Party.*

"Sad Sack" appeared on a different Checker LP called *Bo Diddley* (not the first Checker LP described above.)

Other vintage Checker LPs to look for include: *Boss Man* ("Bo Diddley," "I'm a Man," "Bring It to Jerome," "Hey! Bo Diddley," Diddley Daddy," "Diddy Wah Diddy," "Who Do You Love") and *Bo Diddley's 16 All-Time Greatest Hits* ("Bo Diddley," "Bring It to Jerome," "Hey! Bo Diddley," "I'm a Man" "Diddley Daddy," "Road Runner" "Say Man" "Gun Slinger" "Who Do You Love").